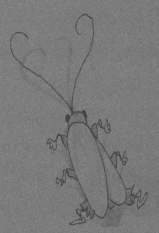

Madame Poulet and Monsieur Roach

Madame Poulet
and
Monsieur Roach

By Dianne de Las Casas
Illustrated by Marita Gentry

PELICAN PUBLISHING COMPANY
Gretna 2009

For Louisiana's children's librarians, under whose wings
I have grown. —D. d. L. C.

For Brent and April. Brent, you rule my roost. April,
you're one cool chick! —M. G.

The word "Pelican" and the depiction of a pelican are trademarks
of Pelican Publishing Company, Inc., and are registered in the
U.S. Patent and Trademark Office.

Library of Congress Cataloging-in-Publication Data

De las Casas, Dianne.
  Madame Poulet and Monsieur Roach / by Dianne de Las Casas ; illustrated by Marita Gentry.
      p. cm.
  Summary: A folktale from New Orleans that explains why cockroaches and chickens are not the best of friends.
  ISBN 978-1-58980-686-3 (hardcover : alk. paper) [1. Folklore—Louisiana—New Orleans. 2. Chickens—Folklore. 3. Cockroaches—Folklore.] I. Gentry, Marita, ill. II. Title.
    PZ8.1.D367Mad 2009
    398.209763'35—dc22

                    2009017021

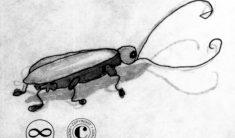

Printed in Korea
Published by Pelican Publishing Company, Inc.
1000 Burmaster Street, Gretna, Louisiana 70053

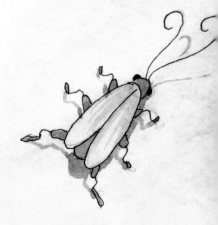

Madame Poulet and Monsieur Roach

Did you know that chickens and cockroaches
were once the very best of friends? That's right,
but it was a very long time ago.

Madame Poulet and Monsieur Roach lived in
a beautiful home. They agreed to contribute to
the household by foraging for food together.

But Monsieur Roach was a *laaaaaaaazy* bug! He did not like hard work and was always thinking of a plan to get out of it.

One morning, Madame Poulet woke up bright and early. She went into the room where Monsieur Roach was lying in bed, and she said, "Monsieur Roach, Monsieur Roach, it's time for us to forage for our food."

But Monsieur Roach pretended to be (cough, cough) sick. He said, "Madame Poulet, I'd love to help you but I think I'm getting sick." (sniffle, cough, sniffle)

Madame Poulet looked at her poor friend lying miserable in bed and said, "Monsieur Roach, Monsieur Roach, it's alright. You stay home, rest, and get better, and I'll forage for our food." Off she went, out the door.

As soon as Madame Poulet was gone, guess what that rascally roach did?

Monsieur Roach hopped out of bed and called all of his roach buddies over. He yelled, "Hey, guys!" The roaches scurried into the house. They began celebrating and had a big cockroach fête, a big party.

Monsieur Roach yelled, "*Laissez les bon temps rouler!* Let the good times roll!" He began to sing and dance.

Madame Poulet, Madame Poulet,
She is gone and that is that.
We will party, we will party,
Until that chicken, she comes back.

Before Madame Poulet returned, all the roaches hurried home. Monsieur Roach hopped back in bed and pretended to be sick.

The next morning, Madame Poulet woke up bright and early. She went into the room where Monsieur Roach was lying in bed, and she said, "Monsieur Roach, Monsieur Roach, it's time for us to forage for our food."

But Monsieur Roach pretended to be (cough, cough) sick. He said, "Madame Poulet, I'd love to help you but today I'm really, really sick." (sniffle, cough, sniffle)

Madame Poulet looked at her poor friend lying miserable in bed and said, "Monsieur Roach, Monsieur Roach, it's alright. You stay home, rest, and get better, and I'll forage for our food." Off she went, out the door.

That's right. He hopped out of bed and called all of his roach buddies over. He yelled, "Hey, guys!" All the roaches scurried into the house. They began celebrating and had a big cockroach fête, a big party.

As soon as Madame Poulet was gone, guess what that roach did?

Monsieur Roach yelled, *"Laissez les bon temps rouler!*
Let the good times roll!"* He began to sing and dance.

Madame Poulet, Madame Poulet,
She is gone and that is that.
We will party, we will party,
Until that chicken, she comes back.

Before Madame Poulet returned, all the roaches hurried home and Monsieur Roach hopped back in bed and pretended to be sick.

On the third day, Madame Poulet woke up bright and early, even earlier than before. She woke up so early that the sun was still sleeping under the horizon. She went into the room where Monsieur Roach was lying in bed, and she said, "Monsieur Roach, Monsieur Roach, it's time for us to forage for our food."

But Monsieur Roach pretended to be (cough, cough) sick. He said, "Madame Poulet, I'd love to help you but I'm really, really, really sick." (sniffle, cough, sniffle)

By this time, Madame Poulet had become a bit suspicious. After all, she was no spring chicken. Madame Poulet looked at her friend differently and said, "Monsieur Roach, Monsieur Roach. You stay home, rest, and get better, and I'll forage for our food." Off she went, out the door.

As soon as Madame Poulet was gone, guess what that rascally roach did?

You know it. Monsieur Roach hopped out of bed and called all of his roach buddies over. He yelled, "Hey, guys!" All the roaches came scurrying into the house. They began celebrating and had a big cockroach fête, a big party.

Monsieur Roach yelled, *"Laissez les bon temps rouler!*
Let the good times roll!"* He began to sing and dance.

Madame Poulet, Madame Poulet,
She is gone and that is that.
We will party, we will party,
Until that chicken, she comes back.

Madame Poulet decided to come home early. As soon as she walked inside the house, she saw . . . *roaches* everywhere!

They were on top of her sofa, on top of her stove, on top of her kitchen table, and even on top of her clean dishes! They were singing and dancing, and there was Monsieur Roach, right in the middle of it, having a good time!

Madame Poulet was furious. She began clucking madly. All the roaches scattered and scurried, looking for a place to hide, looking for a way to escape—but it was too late.

Madame Poulet bent down and slurped up each one of them until they were all gone.

All, that is, except her best friend.

Monsieur Roach cowered in the corner, smiling sheepishly. "Hello, Madame Poulet. How are you?"

Madame Poulet replied, "For three days now, I have been foraging for our food while you have been partying!"

Monsieur Roach smiled sweetly. "Well, would you like to rest now?"

"I don't think so. All that hard work has made me very hungry."

Before Monsieur Roach could
say another word, Madame Poulet
bent down and slurped him up,
just like that.

From that day to this, chickens and roaches are no longer friends. As a matter of fact, if you ever go into a chicken yard, you can still hear the chickens crying, "Roach, roach, roach, roach, roach."

And if the roaches are scurrying by, you can be sure they won't be scurrying by for very long.

So now you know, if you have a problem with roaches, you don't need bug spray. All you need is a chicken.

Foraging for Words

Fête (fet)—French for party or celebration

Forage (FOR-ij)—To search for

Laissez les bon temps rouler! (LEZ-ay leh bon tahm ROO-lay)—French for "Let the good times roll!"

Madame (ma-DAM)—French for "my lady" and similar to ma'am or Mrs.

Monsieur (meh-SYUR)—French for Mr.

Poulet (POO-lay)—French for chicken

Author's Note

I first heard this story told by storyteller Janice Harrington many years ago. Versions of it are related by storytellers around the country. When I discovered that this trickster tale was a New Orleans folktale, I knew I had to tell it myself since I live in the New Orleans area. It has since become one of my most popular tales.

I have written the folktale in a storytelling style. The telling of it should be comical, so take on the characteristics of a chicken when portraying Madame Poulet. Audiences love the interaction between the chicken and the roach. The song that Monsieur Roach sings is to the tune of "La Cucaracha." Have fun with the story and give it your own flair.

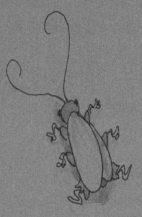